GIVE IT AWAY AND PROSPER!

New Thought for Small Businesses

Beyond the 21st Century Business Model

PAULINE RITCHIE-MOORE

PREFACE

We live in an exciting time! The "Great Shift" has begun and it is up to you to choose which side you want to be on. Yes, it is a choice but the window of opportunity is closing as you are reading this and I want you on board with me which is why I was inspired to look within and present this book offering to you for such a time as this. As a business owner, if you make the active decision to shift with those of us who understand the nature of New Thought for Business, your life will never be the same. How do I know? I know because I am living proof of the principles in this writing that have placed me on the abundant side of this great shift that is taking place right now.

"The Great Shift, you say? I feel that a significant change is taking place but I can't really put my finger on it and it scares me. What does all of this mean for me and my business?"

The Great Shift means just that – the most significant change in the paradigm of our entire Universe that man has ever seen and it's happening right now; the way we do business, who will lead those in business to the next level, the way we sustain ourselves, the way that we help others, the way that we think and the very way that we survive and thrive as human beings on the planet. EVERYTHING that worked in the past is changing...expanding...morphing into something completely different, something greatly intelligent, something like never before, something that you cannot afford to miss or be uninformed about. You have already taken the first step towards your own "great shift" in business...read on.

What makes you an expert on New Thought for Small Businesses?

I am certain that derivatives of doing business this way have been mentioned before, but this way of living the principles of New Thought for Businesses was divinely inspired to me through meditation, performance, and trial and triumph among other things. New Thought for Businesses as written here has never been done before and begs you to test it and see if it won't give you exactly what you need to be your best, most prosperous business self.

My personal journey to inspiration in writing *New Thought For Small Businesses* began when I started my own business in mid-2011. Prior to my completion of a Federal Career Field Internship Program in Prosthetics, I began to feel in my deepest self that a great and wonderful personal shift was about to take place for me. I began to feel that it was time for me to walk in my destiny like never before but not in my current field. As the months went by, the Universe began to conspire on my behalf to make my destiny manifest in the physical. At the time and much to my surprise, the road that I was traveling began to fork and destiny took over. I felt as though I was on autopilot. I was preparing to move to Palo Alto, California for on-the-job training to assume the role of Chief of Prosthetics which seemed like a great plan but in my heart and soul, I knew that the Universe had other plans for me and thus began the guided and inspired changes in my life. I took the steps to make my business official and I felt myself surrender and open up to become a conduit for the Universe to bring forth my destiny. At the time, it didn't feel like all things were working together for my good but I completed my internship and as destiny would have it, the opportunity for my business to flourish came to fruition in place of leaving my family for California and I jumped at the chance. I was offered a local position but I turned it down and left Federal service to continue my ordained journey. For the next year, I tried several good and different business models but none of them felt balanced and well-rounded enough for me. Some of them worked alright, but I wasn't fulfilled. Others worked but the customers weren't as inspired as I knew they could be. And still other ways of doing business worked...or not, because they provided little to no sustenance which meant that I could not help to support my family. So I began to exercise spiritually on a daily basis. This meant meditating, praying, and studying which I paired with good old fashioned hard work. My goal was to be spiritually fit in preparation for my destiny-oriented tasks, both in business and personally. Through spiritual gym time, I began to be inspired not only in my personal life but as I conducted business. During the day, I would go out into the community and introduce people to my products with the goal of sowing inspiration into their lives and at night I would consistently receive and document spiritual revelations on better, more productive and inspiring ways to do business. As I did this, I was given my greatest revelation and the key that connected everything on my life's wish list together. The revelation is this: I was inspired to offer the products as a FREE GIFT! That's right…give the products away. Offer them as a gift to those who believe in the power of a positive word in their lives. Those who agree that the message should be shared can take the gift also or choose it in exchange for a donation of any amount to help continue the work of sowing positively into the lives of others through the affirmations on the products. With this revelation, *New Thought For Businesses* was born! And it has been a boon even with the current depressed economy. In fact, **a down economy has been a huge part of the success of this new way of doing business.** I am given the opportunity to encourage those who need it while growing my business, my network, my finances, and my spiritual life all at once which encompasses by business wish list. My joy overflowed at this revelation and ever since this shift in my way of doing business was inspired to me, my mantra has been this: **Let's all agree never to work another job that does not fulfill our purpose in every way…why else are we here on earth?**

I believe that this model is the future and the key to success for all businesses but in particular, the small business which is the cornerstone of our communities. And it all begins with a desire….to give.

"Give and it shall be given to you, good measure, pressed down, shaken together, and running over shall men give into your bosom".

Why am I so convinced that this will work for your business?

- I am convinced that this will work for you because I have firsthand knowledge of its effectiveness. I developed the principles, tested them, documented the results, tweaked the outcomes, retested them and found that not only did they work, but they were worthy of their calling. As I shared positive, affirming gifts in the form of my products, prosperity attached itself to me. Prosperity for me came in abundance and in several all-important ways: First, customers gave money willingly and cheerfully which is what I needed to continue to grow my business. Second, with almost every transaction, I was told by the customers that the affirmation that was attached to their own personal gift was EXACTLY the confirmation that they needed at the very moment that they needed it. Some were at the point of giving up on their businesses, their marriages, their jobs or job searches, or the positive side of life in general and many just needed a relevant word of confirmation. Time and time again, the affirmation proved to be a much needed inspiration from the Universe that fit their very circumstance like a glove. This is the secret to happy, repeat customers which is every business owner's dream. My energy following each and every product interaction was renewed and so was that of the customers. Customer relationships were reciprocal and for some of them, this was the most positive meaningful exchange they had been a part of all day. This was my hope brought to manifestation. Having witnessed forced, awkward, suspicious sales in the corporate world, I vowed that this would not be standard business practice were it my own company and thanks to my surrendering to the God in me, my path has been anything but forced. Third, I prospered in peace of mind, soul, spirit, and body. Having a way to support myself and the ability to sow seeds into the lives of everyone I met is a priceless gift that I had deeply desired and pursued and finally found, thanks to this new, well-rounded, and divinely inspired way of doing business. Fourth, and as a direct result of the peace and abundance, I gained a new respect from my husband, my daughter, my family and friends. At a time when the economy was and is suffering and people are more unhappy and less prosperous than ever, how ironic is it to find peace, happiness and prosperity in GIVING. And NO! I was not a wealthy housewife with nothing but time and endless resources (blessings to them too)...I was a military wife with very limited resources and a strong spiritual life who was determined to contribute to the world while living my ordained purpose. I started out with $300 in product samples, a willingness to help change the world around me, and an attitude of gratitude and my life was changed.

GIVE IT AWAY AND PROSPER – The Principle

"I can't afford to give away my products! I'm already hurting for money! ". That's what I thought before I discovered that the key to receiving is giving. I had heard about giving many times from "those people with their heads in the clouds" and I could give away a pair of shoes or a few dollars to someone in need, but to give away my products?? Certainly no one expects to keep their heads above water in business by giving away products and services, right? Wrong! Those who understand concepts such as the Law of Attraction, "give and it shall be given unto you", karma, etc., know that the quickest way to prosperity is to give of oneself. This is also true in business and even more so. New thought, forward-wise customers are far more open to giving to socially conscious companies instead of just buying for the vanity of it. People WANT to purchase great products but there must be purpose and sustenance in their giving and they also need to be assured that their purchase is good for them and the environment which is why this new business model is so timely. It contains these qualities and more!

That sounds great but what's in it for me?

From the customer perspective, they receive the following:

a. The customer knows that they are doing business with an ethically and philosophically sound company by purchasing a socially conscious product (the author's company specializes in plant based, fragrance free skin care products that are free of harsh chemicals with the highest safety rating in the industry*) from a socially responsible company. The company matches the customer's expectation and belief.

b. An opportunity to receive positive love and light affirmations that could make their day just a little brighter or propel them into their ordained destiny. Each message carries its own weight and meaning for the receiver.

c. An opportunity to exercise their own free will and feel good about benefiting in every aspect of the product interaction.

d. A product made in an environment where positive energy and good will is integrated into each carefully crafted item which insures a higher quality finished product.

e. The option to receive their personal affirmation for a donation of their choosing, or to receive it for free if they are in need. 99.9% of those we meet always give something if they can. But more importantly, everyone we encounter receives something positive and affirming.

What's in it for you as a business owner:

a. You are perpetuating a cycle of positive social awareness with great products that support a healthy way of life and that of future generations in a responsible manner.

b. You receive donations given in the spirit of good will rather than by pressured sales.

c. You have the rare and wonderful opportunity to work in a self-created environment that merges your positive spiritual life with your everyday work - a luxury that 99% of the population begs for.

d. You also have the exceptional gift of merging your purpose in life (which is to share love and light with others) with a way to support yourself and your family. Inner peace is a side effect of this great life plan.

* FromPermToNatural.com

Who does this plan include and/or exclude:

EVERY PERSON ON THE PLANET can be touched by this business model. Why? Because rich or poor, everyone has the same equal access to affirming products that work. The positive energy that accompanies the spirit of giving forces lives to be optimistically touched by the products or services while the option to give back is theirs alone. Many who have decided to patronize "New Thought" businesses understand that giving to the business is par for the course of receiving bountifully in return. Should the business owner decide to incorporate positive affirmations into the product offerings, not only are the customers lives positively touched but the giver is storing up a treasure trove of goodness that is sure to return to them in high velocity. The amount that is given is a decision made by the receiver with no pressure to barter, scheme, or filch. Those who do not have anything to give at that moment can still be blessed with the gift. It also does not matter the belief system or absence thereof of the receiver. A positive word is always in order. You as a business owner will know that what you are doing makes a difference in the world for those who want for nothing, those in need and everyone in between. As an added bonus, your products are received, seen, used and "paid forward" by far more people than plain old business-as-usual. The vibration of the very atmosphere around you is raised exponentially by the number of customers who feel the same way about your products as you do and want to pass on your message to as many others as they can. It worked for me and I am convinced that it will work for you. It is at this point that I make a 30-day challenge to all business owners. Try this business model for 30 days and watch the abundance of goodness unfold for you and your customers!

I want to start right away...So how do I begin?

No matter what business you are in, you can do this! Begin by searching your current business model for items that you can bless your customers with by either adding them to your existing packages or giving them as stand-alone gifts. For example, If you are a consultant or adviser (doctor, lawyer, etc.), try handing out business card sized affirmations to each client as they enter or leave your place of business. If you make custom or handmade items, find a way to attach positive messages or affirmations of varying kinds to your merchandise. This opens the door for conversations that help customers feel more connected to you. It can also make their day if you have to counsel them on more serious matters. Next, if you would normally sell retail items, then try offering them on a "donation only" basis. This allows the customer to look at the workmanship and care that you have put into your merchandise and usually without fail, they will offer you more in donations than you would normally charge for the item. I have operated using this method and it works. Have faith in people and see that they will not let you down. Give it away in the spirit of love and light and prosper!!

There has been a great paradigm shift in the world of business which presents an amazing opportunity for the small businessperson. In the past, large corporations were the only businesses that could afford to give away everything from trips, to cars, to money. Now, the small business CAN'T afford NOT to give to their customers. This model allows your customers to choose their price and their

peace which makes you BLESSED
TO BE A BLESSING TO OTHERS!

Author's note: Pauline Ritchie-Moore has been a spiritual force from birth. Both her grandparents and parents were spiritual forces in their own rights, having been history making spiritual leaders for more than 60 years combined. Although she has worked in the aerospace and auto industries as an analyst prior to moving into Prosthetics, she knew that her life's purpose was yet to come. She became an ordained and licensed minister and a powerful spirit but as with all powerful spirits, there is always a battle to fight and win to punctuate the power of the SOURCE in the messenger. She has had to fight through personal battles from the bottle to running from her own ordained destiny. She has finally come into her own and this is the second of many divinely inspired writings to be published in direct alignment with her purpose in life. She can be contacted at Ritchie Companies, 350 East Six Forks Road, Suite 150 – #30932, Raleigh, NC 27622. Please be blessed by this offering and enjoy!

www.ingramcontent.com/pod-product-compliance
Lightning Source LLC
Chambersburg PA
CBHW032021190326
41520CB00007B/576